Please return/renew this item by the last date
shown. Books may be renewed by
telephoning, writing to or calling in at any
library or on the Internet.

Northamptonshire Libraries and Information Service

**Northamptonshire**
**County Council**

www.northamptonshire.gov.uk/leisure/libraries/

60  000  116  639

# weblinks

You don't need a computer to use this book. But, for readers who do have access to the Internet, the book provides links to recommended websites which offer additional information and resources on the subject.

You will find weblinks boxes like this on some pages of the book.

## weblinks

For more information about a specific topic here, go to www.waylinks.co.uk/series/ religiontoday/Islam

## waylinks.co.uk

To help you find the recommended websites easily and quickly, weblinks are provided on our own website, **waylinks.co.uk.** These take you straight to the relevant websites and save you typing in the Internet address yourself.

## Website content

## Internet safety

↗ Never give out personal details, which include: your name, address, school, telephone number, email address, password and mobile number.

↗ Do not respond to messages which make you feel uncomfortable – tell an adult.

↗ Do not arrange to meet in person someone you have met on the Internet.

↗ Never send your picture or anything else to an online friend without a parent's or teacher's permission.

↗ If you see anything that worries you, tell an adult.

### A note to adults
Internet use by children should be supervised. We recommend that you install filtering software which blocks unsuitable material.

The weblinks for this book are checked and updated regularly. However, because of the nature of the Internet, the content of a website may change at any time, or a website may close down without notice. While the Publishers regret any inconvenience this may cause readers, they cannot be responsible for the content of any website other than their own.

WAYLAND

# Islam

## Gianna Quaglia

WAYLAND

First published in 2007 by Wayland

Copyright © Wayland 2007
This book is based on *21st Century Islam* by David Self
originally published by Wayland.

Wayland
338 Euston Road
London NW1 3BH

Wayland Australia
Hachette Children's Books
Level 17/207 Kent Street
Sydney, NSW 2000

Subject consultant: Dr Fatma Amer, consultant in Islamic
Education and Inter Faith Relations

Maps and artwork: Peter Bull

All rights reserved.

British Library Cataloguing Publication Data
Quaglia, Gianna
  Islam. - (World religions today)
  1. Islam - Juvenile literature
  I. Title
  297

ISBN 978 07502 5266 9

Printed in China

Wayland is a division of Hachette Children's Books,
an Hachette Livre UK company

| Northamptonshire Libraries & Information Service | |
| --- | --- |
| 60 000 116 639 | |
| Peters | 17-Mar-2011 |
| 297 | £12.99 |
| | |

The publisher would like to thank the following for permission
to reproduce their pictures: Christophe Boisvieux/Corbis
covers; The Art Archive /Turkish and Islamic Art Museum
Istanbul/Harper Collins Publishers 8, Dagli Orti 31;
Bridgeman Art Library www.bridgeman.co.uk/University
Library, Istanbul, Turkey 38; Corbis/SUPRI/Reuters 44;
Hutchison Picture Library 29; Impact Photos 4; Alex Keene
26; Ann and Bury Peerless 12, 39, 41; Peter Sanders
Photography Ltd 6, 7, 9, 18, 19, 20, 23, 24, 28, 30, 32, 34,
35, 36, 37, 40; Topfoto 11, 13, 14, 15, 16, 17, 21, 22, 25, 33,
42, 43, 45

# Contents

Introduction                                      4

1 The growth of Islam                             6

2 Muslim beliefs and teachings                   16

3 How Muslims worship                            22

4 Muslim life                                    32

5 Islam today                                    42

  Glossary                                       46

  Timeline and further reading                   47

  Index                                          48

## Note

*When Muslims use the name of their Prophet, they usually follow it with the blessing 'Peace be upon him' – shown in Arabic as: The Prophet Muhammad* ﷺ

*In the Western world years are numbered as either* BC *('Before Christ') or* AD *(Anno Domini – which is Latin for 'In the year of our Lord…'). In this book, the more neutral terms* BCE *('Before the Common Era') and* CE *('Common Era') are used.*

Northamptonshire DISCARDED Libraries

# Introduction

Muslims are the followers of the religion Islam. For Muslims, the most important teacher in the world is the Prophet Muhammad ﷺ.

## One God

The **Prophet** Muhammad ﷺ was born in Makkah, in what is now Saudi Arabia. He worked as a shepherd and trader. At the age of 40 an angel began to visit him, giving him messages from God which he was to repeat to his followers. These messages were the teachings of Islam.

They were later collected to form the Muslim holy book, the **Qur'an**. Muslims believe the Qur'an is the word of God, written in its own style of **Arabic**.

The most important message of the Qur'an is that there is only one God, whose name in Arabic is 'Allah'.

## Islam

The teaching that the Prophet Muhammad ﷺ brought to his people is known as Islam, which means 'peace and submission', or 'obedience to God'. The followers of Islam are called Muslims. For Muslims, the Prophet did not start a new religion. He taught the same

**weblinks**
For more information about Islam, go to
www.waylinks.co.uk/series/
religiontoday/Islam

◄ *The star and crescent moon are popular symbols in Islamic art.*

message as other prophets including Noah, Ibrahim (Abraham), Musa (Moses) and Isa (Jesus): that there is only one true God.

## Islam worldwide

Islam is now the second largest religion in the world, with about 1.3 billion Muslims living in almost every country. Many Muslims live in the north of Africa and the Middle East, as well as in central Africa, Indonesia, China and Russia. Many Muslims have also settled in Europe. For example, there are about 1.5 million Muslims living in Britain.

## Countries with the largest Muslim populations

| Country | Number of Muslims |
|---|---|
| Indonesia | 170 million |
| Pakistan | 136 million |
| Bangladesh | 106 million |
| India | 103 million |
| Turkey | 62 million |
| Iran | 60 million |
| Egypt | 53 million |
| Nigeria | 47 million |
| China | 37 million |

▼ This map shows where Muslims live.

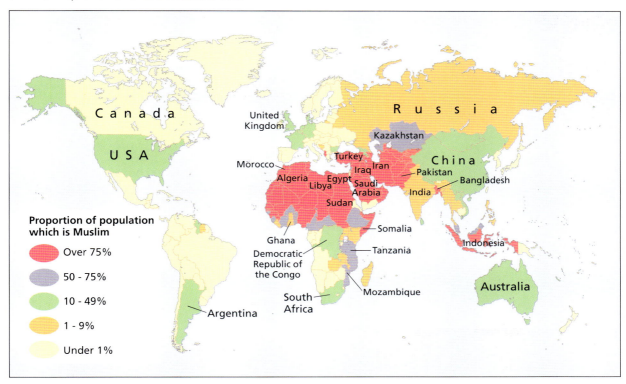

# 1 ★ The growth of Islam

Islam teaches that there is only one God – a God who has made everything, knows everything and sees everything.

## The Prophet of Islam

Muhammad ﷺ lived in the city of Makkah in what is now Saudi Arabia from 570CE until 632. His father died before he was born and his mother died when he was six, so he was looked after by his grandfather and later by an uncle. He came from a poor but important family. When he grew up, he worked for his uncle who was a trader. Later, Muhammad ﷺ worked for a wealthy widow called Khadijah, who also lived in Makkah. Eventually Khadijah and Muhammad ﷺ married. They had six children.

▼ *The Great Mosque of Makkah, and the modern city beyond its walls.*

## Ghar Hira

At that time, the people of Makkah were leading **immoral** lives. There was fighting, drinking and poverty. Many people worshipped statues or **idols** made of stone or wood. Muhammad ﷺ was very worried about what he saw in Makkah. He often walked out of the city to Jabal al-Nour (the 'Mountain of Light') and spent his time praying and wondering how he could help his people. His favourite spot was a place called Ghar Hira.

## The Angel Jibril

One night, when Muhammad ﷺ was in Ghar Hira, he heard a voice. He saw the Angel Jibril (also known as Gabriel). The angel asked Muhammad ﷺ to repeat his words until he learnt them by heart.

After that, the Angel Jibril appeared often to Muhammad ﷺ, giving him many messages for the people of Makkah – especially the message that there is only one God, whose name is Allah. Everything the angel told Muhammad ﷺ was later written in the Qur'an.

➤ *This is the place where the Prophet is said to have been visited by the Angel Jibril.*

## Makkah

The Prophet started to teach the people of Makkah what the angel had told him. Many listened and became followers of these teachings. But there were many people who did not like the Prophet's message about One God. The rulers of Makkah tried to starve the Prophet and his family to death. When that failed, they tried to stop people trading with his family. After two years, they decided to kill Muhammad ﷺ. Muhammad ﷺ and his faithful friend and companion, Abu Bakr, escaped. They found a cave to hide in.

## The spider's web

Inside the cave, the Prophet and Abu Bakr heard their enemy coming closer. Then a miracle happened. When they got to the cave, their enemies saw a spider's web that covered the entrance. Above it, a grey dove sat singing on a branch. They thought nobody could have entered the cave and they moved on.

## Al Hijrah

The Prophet and Abu Bakr crossed the desert to Madinah. They were welcomed by the people. The first **mosque** was built in Madinah.

Eight years later, in 630CE, the Prophet was able to return to Makkah. There most of the people became Muslims. All the idols were removed from a holy place called the **Ka'bah**, which Muslims believe was the first house ever built for the worship of the One God.

The Muslim calendar starts from the day the Prophet left Makkah (16 July 622CE) on his journey to Madinah. The event is celebrated every year as *Al Hijrah,* which means 'the journey'. It is the first day of the Muslim year.

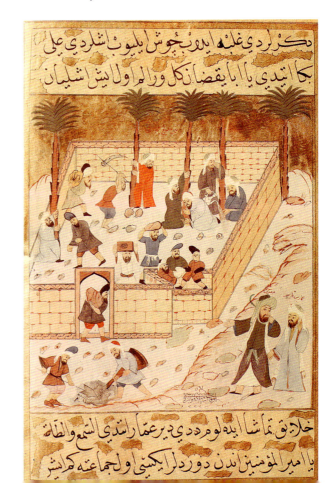

## The Ka'bah

The Ka'bah is a building in the shape of a cube. Muslims believe the first Ka'bah was built by the first man, Adam, after he had been sent away from the Garden of Eden, as a house where he could praise God. Later, a man Muslims call Ibrahim (and whom Jews and Christians call Abraham) built a new Ka'bah in the same place. After many years, the Ka'bah was used to worship idols. Then the Prophet Muhammad ﷺ once again made it a place for worship of the One God. (See page 30 for more about the Ka'bah.)

➤ Muslim pilgrims visit the Ka'bah.

◀ This painting shows the building of the Prophet's mosque in Madinah. The Prophet helped build it and lived next to it. The painting dates from the 18th century.

## The Muslim calendar

Islamic years are counted from the Hijrah (AH means 'After the Hijrah'), when the Prophet left Makkah. This was on 16 July 622CE. There are roughly 103 Muslim years to every 100 Western years.

This is because the Muslim calendar follows the cycles of the moon. It takes the moon about 29 or 30 days to go around the earth.

The Western calendar is worked out according to the sun. A Western year is about 365 days, which is how long it takes the earth to go once around the sun.

## The four khalifahs

The Prophet Muhammad ﷺ died in 632CE. His friend and son-in-law Abu Bakr became his **successor** and the leader of Islam. The Arabic word for successor is *khalifah* (or caliph). Abu Bakr ruled for two years until he died. Then another of the Prophet's companions, Umar, ruled for ten years. He was killed in 644CE.

Before he died, Umar set up a council that would choose the next khalifah. It suggested two men, Uthman bin Affan and Ali bin Talib, both sons-in-law of the Prophet. Uthman was elected. He ruled for twelve years until he was killed in 656CE.

Ali, who was the Prophet's cousin as well as his son-in-law, became the fourth khalifah. He wrote many speeches, sermons and letters. But in 661CE, he too was killed.

These first four khalifahs are known as the *rashidun*, or 'rightly guided'; that is, they were seen as God's representatives on earth.

## The spread of Islam

By the year 732CE, Muslims ruled from Spain to India, including the south of France, northern Africa, Egypt and much of the Middle East. There were different rulers in each place, but they all spoke Arabic and had laws based on the Qur'an.

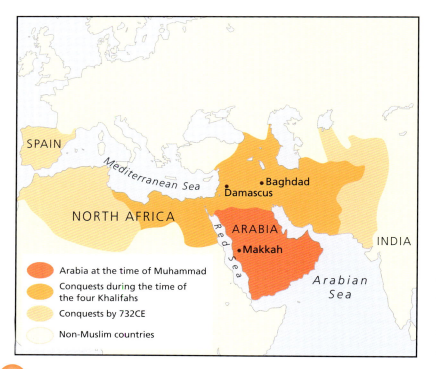

SPAIN

Mediterranean Sea

•Baghdad
Damascus

NORTH AFRICA

Red Sea

ARABIA

•Makkah

INDIA

Arabian Sea

Arabia at the time of Muhammad

Conquests during the time of the four Khalifahs

Conquests by 732CE

Non-Muslim countries

◄ This map shows the spread of Islam after the death of the Prophet. By the time of Umar, Muslims ruled from Libya in the west to Afghanistan in the east, as well as what became known as Arabia.

## Shi'ah and Sunni

When the Prophet died, there were people who wanted Ali (see page 10) to be khalifah. They wanted all future leaders of Islam to come from the Prophet's family. These supporters became known as the Shi'at-Ali, which means 'the party of Ali'. Today they are known as **Shi'ah** Muslims. They live mainly in Iran and southern Iraq.

Shi'ahs believe that their leaders, called **imams**, are guided by God and should be descended from the Prophet. They are now led by teachers called **ayatollahs**, and have other priests and teachers who explain hidden meanings in the Qur'an.

About 90 per cent of Muslims belong to a group called the **Sunnis**. They take their name from the **Sunnah**, a Muslim holy book. Like the Shi'ahs, Sunni Muslims follow the teachings of the Prophet and believe that the Qur'an shows them the way to live. They respect Muslim teachers called imams, but Sunnis do not have any special priests.

➤ Although most Muslims in Pakistan are Sunnis, there are also many Shi'ahs. Here Shi'ahs carry black flags at the festival of Ashura (see pages 26 and 27), in memory of the **martyrdom** of al-Husain ibn Ali, son of the fourth khalifah, Ali.

11

## Jerusalem

Problems between Islamic countries and Christian countries began early on. Jerusalem is a holy city for Jews and Christians as well as Muslims. Jerusalem was captured by the second khalifah, Umar, in 638CE. In 1099, Christian armies captured it back from Muslims during one of many **crusades**.

The Muslims re-captured the city in 1187. Their leader Salah-ad-Din (sometimes known as Saladin) made peace with King Richard I of England. But the crusades continued throughout the 13th and 14th centuries.

➤ *The Dome of the Rock (Qubbat al-Sakhra) in Jerusalem is sacred to Jews and Muslims.*

## Powerful empires

All this time, the Muslim world gained in power and wealth. One important Muslim empire was the Ottoman Empire, which lasted from about 1300 to 1920. Based in what is now Turkey, at one time this empire stretched from Algeria in Africa to Basra in Iraq, and north to include Hungary and parts of Russia. Its greatest ruler was Emperor Suleiman, who ruled in the 16th century. At about the same time, another powerful Muslim empire, that of the Mughals, stretched across India.

Both Mughal and Ottoman Empires were centres of vast wealth, luxury and learning.

## The Mughals

The mighty Mughal Empire was founded by Babur in 1526. Babur became ruler of Turkestan when he was twelve and later conquered Afghanistan. In 1525 he invaded India and conquered large areas of the country in two years.

Babur's grandson, Akbar (ruled 1556-1605), doubled the area under Muslim control, so that the Mughal Empire stretched across almost all of what is now India and Pakistan. Akbar built great palaces at Delhi and Agra.

The Mughal Empire was attacked by the Persians (now Iranians) in 1739 and during the 19th century the British gradually took control of the country. The Mughal Empire ended in 1858.

➤ This painting of the Mughal court shows two Christian priests visiting the Emperor Akbar.

## Ruled by the West

For 250 years, from about 1700 to 1950, large parts of the Muslim world came under Western rule. Many Muslim countries became **colonies** in empires ruled from Britain, France and the Netherlands. Western governments were not always respectful of Muslim traditions. Islamic treasures were taken back to Western cities.

## Independence

In the 20th century, Muslim countries became independent. In Arabia, for example, the Islamic kingdom of Saudi Arabia was founded in 1926.

Many Muslim countries became independent after the Second World War. In 1947, India was divided into two separate countries – Pakistan and India. Many Muslims headed for Pakistan, which was mainly a Muslim country. Many **Hindus** headed in the opposite direction, to India. There were fights between the groups when they met on the way.

◄ These oilfields in Kuwait supply fuel to the Western world. Saddam Hussein of Iraq invaded this area in 1990.

The discovery of oil has brought new wealth to some Muslim countries, particularly in the Middle East. Since then, some people in these countries have turned against Western culture. They want laws based on Islamic values.

## Sufis

*Sufis are Muslims who try to become as close to God as possible by leading a very simple way of life. They were called Sufis because they wore long woollen robes, called* sufs. *Sufis chant or perform rhythmic, whirling dances to try to achieve a closeness with God.*

▼ *A 'whirling dervish'. Sufis spin in order to become one with God.*

# 2 ★ Muslim beliefs and teachings

For all Muslims, Islam is based on the Qur'an. The Qur'an tells Muslims what they should believe and how they should live their lives. Muslims treat the Qur'an with great respect.

### The Qur'an

The Prophet Muhammad ﷺ could not read or write. Each time the Angel Jibril revealed God's teachings to him, Muhammad ﷺ learned them by heart. Immediately after, he repeated them to his friends. They wrote them down on anything they could find – paper, leather, even pieces of bone.

▼ *These two pages from a 17th-century Qur'an are beautifully decorated.*

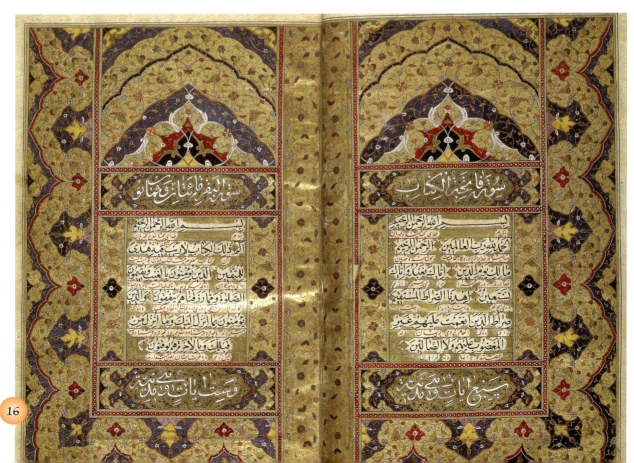

## Translating the Qur'an

*The Qur'an is written in classical Arabic. Nowadays millions of Muslims do not speak Arabic, so the Qur'an has been been translated into many different languages. Because Muslims believe that the Arabic text of the Qur'an is the actual word of God, they believe that no translation can ever replace the original version.*

*Arabic letters are different from Western ones. Sometimes, different English spellings are used to imitate the sound of an Arabic word – which is why the word 'Qur'an' is sometimes spelt 'Koran' in English.*

▼ *Young Muslim girls in the Philippines memorise sections of the Qur'an by heart.*

The third khalifah, Uthman, ordered a man called Zaid ibn Thabit and a team of **scribes** to collect all the sayings. The sayings were written down exactly as the Prophet had repeated them, to form the Qur'an. Since then, the words of the Qur'an have never been changed.

The Qur'an contains 114 chapters called *surahs*. Each surah (except surah 9) begins with the words: 'In the name of Allah, the compassionate, the merciful.' These words are called the *Bismillah*. Muslims say the Bismillah before eating or doing any important job. The Qur'an must only be touched with clean hands.

## The teachings of Islam

Muslims respect the holy books of Jews and Christians, but they believe that the Qur'an is God's final and complete teaching. It is a book of teachings, laws and wise sayings.

The shorter chapters, or surahs, were mostly revealed in Makkah, before the Prophet moved to Madinah. Nearly all of these surahs teach Muslims about the oneness of God, about creation and life after death. These surahs also speak of the greatness and mercy of God.

▼ *Young students of an Islamic school in London wear headscarves and modest dress.*

The Angel Jibril instructed that the longer surahs should come at the beginning of the Qur'an. These longer surahs were revealed in Madinah after the first Muslim state was founded. They tell Muslims how to live their lives based on equality and justice. They include laws about how to run the state, as well as tell Muslims to dress modestly and not to be greedy.

## The Sunnah

Everything the Prophet Muhammad ﷺ did was written down, so Muslims know how he spoke, slept, dressed and walked. This is called the *Sirah*. Some years after the death of the

▲ Two Muslim boys at Qur'an School in Mauritania, in western Africa. Even though they speak a dialect called Hansaniya Arabic, they learn the Qur'an on their tablets in classical Arabic.

Prophet, all his sayings were collected together. All the sayings that were agreed to be genuine were included. This book is called the *Hadith*. Hadith means 'statement'.

Together, the Sirah and the Hadith are called the Sunnah. The word means 'method' or 'example'. Muslims try to live in the way shown by the Qur'an and the Sunnah.

## Some sayings of the Prophet

*'God does not look upon your bodies and appearances. He looks upon your hearts and deeds.'*

*'God is gentle and loves gentleness in all things.'*

## The Shahadah

Muslims all around the world learn that the first duty of Islam is to say the **Shahadah**:

'There is no god but God and Muhammad is his Prophet.'

It is by saying this (and believing it) that a person becomes a Muslim.

Muslims believe in all the prophets that came before Muhammad ﷺ, such as Nuh (Noah), Ibrahim (Abraham), Musa (Moses) and Isa (Jesus). They respect Isa (Jesus) as one of God's prophets.

## Learning the Qur'an

Muslims believe that the Qur'an is the most important book in the world, and many Muslims learn large sections of the Qur'an by heart. Schools in many Muslim countries teach the Qur'an. In non-Muslim countries, children often go to special classes after their ordinary school day has finished.

Some Muslims learn the whole Qur'an by heart. Anyone who can do this is highly respected. They are given the title *hafiz*.

▼ *The Shahadah written in Arabic.*

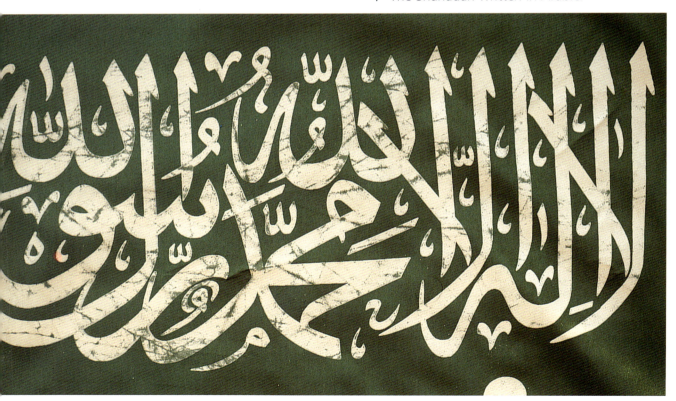

## The 'Five Pillars' of Islam

*Islam has five rules or 'pillars'. They are called pillars because they help a Muslim to live a good life – in the same way that pillars support a building. They are mentioned in the Qur'an:*

**1** Shahadah or *making a statement of faith*

**2** Salah or *prayer (see pages 22-3)*

**3** Zakah or *helping the needy (see pages 36-7)*

**4** Sawm or **fasting** *(see page 28)*

**5** Hajj or **pilgrimage** *(see pages 30-1)*

*Other rules in the Qur'an teach Muslims to be honest and generous; never to eat pork or to drink alcohol, and never to gamble. Muslims must also be ready to fight for justice.*

▼ *Young boys in Karachi, Pakistan, go to a special school to learn to recite the Qur'an.*

# How Muslims worship

**M**uslims believe that their whole lives should be lived for God. Prayer is one of the five rules, or 'pillars', of the Muslim faith.

◄ *A Muslim in Thata, Pakistan, washes before praying.*

### Prayer

One of the five duties of a Muslim is prayer. The Qur'an says it is important to pray at set times.

Muslims pray five times a day, at the times taught by the Prophet. These five set times are:

- between the first sign of day and sunrise
- between just after midday and just after mid-afternoon
- between just after mid-afternoon and just after sunset
- between just after sunset and before it goes dark
- when it is dark

Muslims can pray anywhere that is clean – provided they are also clean. This special act of washing before prayer is called *wudu*.

To pray, Muslims must face in the direction of the Ka'bah (see page 9). They say their prayers in Arabic.

There are different positions for each part of the prayer. First, a Muslim stands to show he is listening to God. Then he bows to show respect to God. Next he bows low twice, touching the ground with forehead, knees, nose and palms. Between each of these low bows, he sits back on his heels. All the movements are repeated two, three or four times according to the time of day. Muslims also say their own private prayers in their own language.

## The Exordium

*When they pray, Muslims repeat the first words of the Qur'an:*

*'In the name of God,*
*The most Gracious,*
*The most Merciful,*
*All praise be to God alone, the Lord of Creation,*
*The most Gracious, the most Merciful*
*King of Judgement Day!*
*You alone we worship and to You alone we pray for help.*
*Guide us in the right way – the way of those you have blessed, not the way of those that have been condemned by you or of those who go astray.'*

➤ *Muslims pray together at the Islamia School in Brent, in north London, UK.*

## Going to the mosque

The place where Muslims gather together to worship God is called a mosque. Many mosques have a tall tower called a minaret. Five times a day, at the set times, a man called a *mu'adhin* (sometimes spelt muezzin) traditionally calls Muslims from the minaret to pray to God. The most important prayers of the week are those said after midday on a Friday. At this time, Muslim men go to a mosque to pray together. Women may also go, but many prefer to pray at home.

In each mosque, there is a place where Muslims may wash so that they are not dirty when they pray to God. They also take off their shoes before entering the prayer hall inside the mosque. There are no chairs or seats in the main prayer hall. Instead, the floor is always covered with carpets.

In each mosque, there is an arch (called a *mihrab*) on one wall which

▼ *The New Federal Mosque in Kuala Lumpur, Malaysia, was opened in 2000 and can hold up to 17,000 worshippers at one time.*

shows the direction of the Ka'bah. The person leading the prayers may stand in front of the mihrab.

Muslim law says that wherever forty Muslim men live in the same area, they should hold Friday prayers together. Many mosques are impressive buildings. There are never any statues or pictures in a mosque.

Besides the main Prayer Hall, there may be a separate area where women can pray. In some mosques, men and women pray in the same hall.

## The khateeb

*At Friday prayers, there is usually a khutbah or a talk. This is usually given by the* khateeb, *a leader chosen by other Muslims at that mosque.*

**weblinks**

For more information about going to the mosque, go to www.waylinks.co.uk/series/religiontoday/Islam

➤ *Muslim men attend a mosque in New York. They sit facing the mihrab (arch) in the direction of the Ka'bah. To the right of the mihrab, the khateeb gives his sermon (khutbah).*

## Festivals and holy days

The most important Muslim festivals are Id-ul-Fitr and Id-ul-Adha ('Id', or 'Eid', means 'festival'; see page 28). But Muslims celebrate many other special days each year.

### Al Hijrah

This festival, which is on New Year's Day in the Islamic calendar, recalls when the Prophet Muhammad ﷺ moved from Makkah to Madinah.

### Ashura

Shi'ah Muslims remember the martyrdom of al-Husain ibn Ali, a grandson of the Prophet, in 680CE.

### Maulid al-Nabi

This festival celebrates the Prophet's birthday.

### Laylat-al-Mi'raj (The Night Journey)

This festival celebrates the 'Night Journey' made by the Prophet Muhammad ﷺ with the Angel Jibril. They went from Makkah to Jerusalem on a winged horse in a single night.

### Ramadan

Ramadan is the month of fasting (see pages 28-9).

### Laylat-ul-Qadr (The Night of Power)

This festival marks the night when the Qur'an was first revealed to the Prophet by the Angel Jibril. Many Muslims spend the night reading the Qur'an or praying in their local mosque.

**weblinks**

For more information about going to the mosque, go to www.waylinks.co.uk/series/religiontoday/Islam

◄ *A selection of Id (or Eid) cards which Muslims send out at the end of Ramadan.*

## The Islamic months

*Islam has its own calendar based on the moon. The Western calendar is worked out according to how long it takes the earth to go around the sun, which is just over 365 days. The Islamic calendar has twelve months of 29 or 30 days long (the time between one new moon and the next). This means that a Muslim year is about eleven days shorter than a Western year. So Muslim holy days are always on different days of the Western calendar. Islamic months begin at sunset when the first new moon is seen in a certain place.*

| Islamic months | Festivals (with date) |
|---|---|
| Muharram | 1 Al Hijrah (Prophet's journey to Madinah) |
| | 10 Ashura |
| Safar | |
| Rabi' al-Awwal | 12 Maulid al-Nabi (The Birthday of the Prophet) |
| Rabi' ath-Thani | |
| Jamadi al-Awwal | |
| Jamadi al-Akhir | |
| Rajab | 27 Laylat-al-Mi'raj (The Night Journey) |
| Sha'ban | |
| Ramadan | 27 Laylat-ul-Qadr (The Night of Power) |
| Shawwal | 1 Id-ul-Fitr (Day after Ramadan) |
| Dhul-Qa'da | |
| Dhul-Hijja | Al Hajj (Pilgrimage to Makkah) |
| | 10 Id-ul-Adha (End of the Hajj) |

# Ramadan

Ramadan is the ninth month of the Muslim year. It is special because it is the month when the Prophet first received teachings from the Angel Jibril. Muslims fast for thirty days. They don't eat, drink or smoke from dawn until sunset.

During this month, Muslims are also meant to say extra prayers and to try to read the whole of the Qur'an. All healthy adult Muslims are expected to fast. Most children try to fast once they reach the age of twelve. Ramadan is also a time for giving to charity.

▲ *A British Muslim family share their evening meal after their daily fast during the month of Ramadan.*

Before sunrise, during Ramadan, Muslims have a meal called *suhoor*. They eat foods such as bread with olive oil, rice or porridge, boiled eggs or fruit. After sunset, they end that day's fast with *iftar*, milk, a few dates or nuts and savoury pastries.

## Id-ul-Fitr

The day after Ramadan is a big celebration. It begins with an early meal. Then everyone puts on their best clothes and goes to the mosque. Later, they visit relatives and friends to swap presents and cards, and give each other sweets.

## Id-ul-Adha

This festival marks the end of the Hajj, when Muslims go to Makkah. It is celebrated by all Muslims and not just those who go on pilgrimage. An animal (a sheep, goat, cow or even a camel) is killed, and its meat is shared between the family, friends and the poor. This is done in memory of when Ibrahim (Abraham) almost **sacrificed** his son to God.

## In our own words

*"I fast not because food is bad or eating is wicked. I fast because going without food all day makes me really enjoy my evening meal. A meal at the end of the day's fast is something I really look forward to. I also fast to remind myself that many people are too poor to eat. Fasting makes me not give in, the moment I feel hungry. It helps make my mind stronger than my body"*

Zulfiquar, aged 13, UK

▼ *In Jakarta, Indonesia, Muslims gather for early morning prayers on Id-ul-Fitr, the day after Ramadan.*

## The Hajj

The fifth duty or pillar of Islam is to make a pilgrimage to Makkah. The word for this duty is 'Hajj'. The Hajj happens during the second week of the twelfth month of the Muslim year.

The city of Makkah (in Saudi Arabia) is important to Muslims not only because it was the birthplace of Muhammad ﷺ, but also because it is the site of the Ka'bah, their holiest place. Today, the Ka'bah stands in the courtyard of the Great Mosque of Makkah. It is covered in a black cloth with the words of the Qur'an embroidered upon it.

As the pilgrims approach Makkah, they stop to put on special clothes. For a man, this is two pieces of white, unsewn cloth. The reason is so that you cannot tell who is important or rich. Everyone looks the same and is equal. Women must not cover their faces.

▼ During the Hajj, pilgrims live in a vast tented city near Makkah.

Pilgrims walk seven times round the Ka'bah. Then they walk between the two hills of Safa and Marwah nearby. This is done in memory of Hajar (said to be an ancestor of all Muslim people) who searched in this desert place for water for her son. It is said that God caused a spring to gush out of the ground. Pilgrims take home water from the spring.

The most important part of the Hajj is when pilgrims go to the nearby Plain of Arafat where Muhammad ﷺ preached his last sermon. Next they go to Mina. Here they throw stones at three pillars in memory of how Ibrahim once rejected the devil. The pilgrims then return to the Ka'bah.

▼ *This home, in Egypt, has been decorated to show that its owner has been to Makkah.*

# 4★ Muslim life

**B**eing Muslim is not just about saying prayers, going to the mosque and feasting or fasting at special times. The Qur'an and the teachings of the Prophet tell a Muslim how to live each day.

## Family life

For Muslims, the family is very important. As soon as a baby is born, its father whispers into its ear the Shahadah: 'There is no god but God and Muhammad is his Prophet.' In this way, the very first words the baby hears are about God and his Prophet. By hearing these words the baby is welcomed into the faith.

**— weblinks ▸ —**

For more information about life as a Muslim, go to www.waylinks.co.uk/series/religiontoday/Islam

◄ *A father whispers the Shahadah to his baby.*

Muslim children are taught about their faith and how to pray from a young age. As Muslim children get older, they are expected to work hard at school and to help with jobs at home.

There are rules to guide Muslims when it comes to making friends and spending time outdoors. All teenagers are expected to show respect to older people. Once they are grown-up, children are expected to care for their parents as they reach old age. Muslims often live in large family groups and members of the family help each other at all times.

Family life is so important for Muslims that much of the home may be kept private from outsiders. Visitors will be shown to a guest room. They will meet the men and boys of the family. The women and girls may stay in another room where they invite their female guests.

Muslims also believe that all believers belong to the family of Islam, whatever their skin colour, and that they should help others who are poor by giving *zakah*, or charity.

▼ *A Muslim family in Denmark celebrates the end of Ramadan – the festival of Id-ul-Fitr.*

## Marriage

Family life is sacred in Islam. That is why the Qur'an encourages all Muslims to marry and have children. The relationship between husband and wife should be based on love and mercy. Parents should do their best to care for their children and be kind and loving to them. Children learn how to respect and honour their parents as well as other elderly members in their family.

Before a Muslim wedding takes place, the couple agree rules for their marriage and these rules are written down and signed. There is usually a wedding party.

## Divorce

Muslims can get divorced if the marriage fails completely. If they divorce, the wife receives some money from her ex-husband and keeps all their household goods. The couple are free to remarry.

◄ *In Pakistan, a Muslim bride and groom wear traditional dress. Music and feasting will follow for the rest of the day and long into the night.*

## Arranged marriages

Muslim marriages are often 'arranged' by parents and older relatives. It is often said that parents can tell who would make a good life-long partner for their child better than the young person can. Most young Muslims are happy to follow their family's choice – but today some young Muslims (especially those living in Western countries) want to make their own choices. Even where a wedding is 'arranged', a young person still has the right to refuse the person their parents have chosen. Islamic law forbids forced marriages.

◄ *Not every Muslim couple wears traditional dress for their marriage ceremony. This Chinese couple have just got married in Mongolia.*

## Zakah

Zakah (sometimes spelt zakat) is one of the 'pillars' of Islam. It is like a tax. Anyone who can afford to, has to give money or food to the poor. Money may be given to help people who have suffered from a disaster such as an earthquake, or to help with the building of a hospital or mosque – or to help a poor student to study at a college or university.

▼ *Two elders and an imam at a mosque in Buckinghamshire, UK, work out how the zakah should be handed out.*

Muslims believe that everything they own really belongs to God. They also believe that God will judge how each Muslim uses what he or she has been given. Giving zakah reminds Muslims of this teaching.

There are rules about how much zakah should be paid. Crops, herds of animals and money in a bank all count as part of a person's wealth. Homes, clothes and furniture do not.

▲ *Women in Fes, Morocco, meet together to learn and study the meaning of the Qur'an.*

## The rich man and the poor man

Muslims are taught to be generous – as this story or parable shows:

There was once a poor man who owed a rich man money. The poor man offered to pay the rich man back a little at a time. "Very well. Pay me when you can," said the rich man.

This rich man will be rewarded by God for being kind. But the story goes on to show that it would have been better if the rich man had said:

"Forget what you owe me: it will be my zakah."

## Knowledge

The Prophet once said that it was the duty of every Muslim, male or female, to learn. The desire to learn new things led Muslims to build the first universities, public libraries and public hospitals. The oldest university in the world opened in Cairo in Egypt in 970CE. But some Muslims think the Prophet meant they should only learn about religion.

## Mathematics

What we usually call Arabic numerals (1, 2, 3, and so on) originally came from India where they were developed by Hindu thinkers. Muslim mathematicians invented the way we do basic arithmetic. In Roman times, Europeans used the numbers I, II, III, IV and so on, which are more difficult to use in sums. Slowly the West began to use Arabic numerals instead. It also copied the Arabic system of working out addition and subtraction sums from right to left (Arabic writing is read from right to left too).

◄ This 16th-century painting shows Muslim astronomers in Turkey, as they calculate the size of the universe and the movements of the planets.

► The walls of the Wazir Khan mosque in Lahore, Pakistan are covered with decorated tilework, using geometric and floral patterns as well as beautiful writing.

## Science

A Muslim astronomer called al-Biruni (973-1048) calculated the time it takes the earth to go round the sun (he was 24 seconds out), five hundred years before anyone in the West could. He worked out that the earth turns once a day. Another Muslim scientist called Ibn Sina (980-1037; also known as Avicenna) wrote a 24-volume medical encyclopaedia which became the most important medical text for 700 years. Muslims also invented the compass, test tubes and surgical instruments, water mills and windmills – and the guitar.

## Art

The Prophet taught that the worship of statues or idols is wrong, so there are never any paintings or statues of animals or people in mosques and in holy books. Muslim artists became experts in designs using flowers, plants and patterns. These patterns decorate the walls of mosques and other buildings all over the world.

Muslims think that beautiful handwriting is the greatest form of art, because it is used to write out words from the Qur'an. Words from the Qur'an have often been used to decorate walls and ceramics.

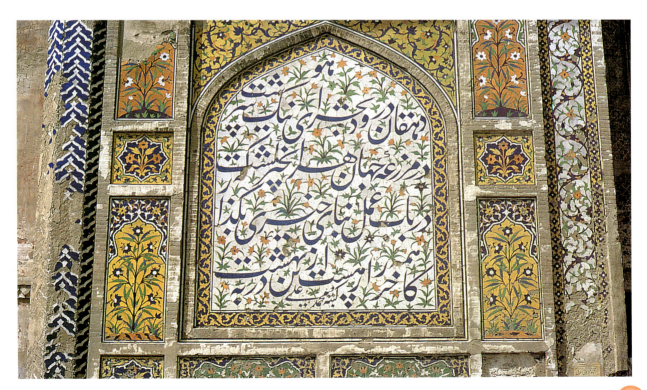

*Islam*

## Death

Muslims try to make sure that nobody dies alone. The body is washed by the family (a man's body by the men, a woman's by the women) and is wrapped in white sheets. (The body of a person who has died in battle is not washed.) The body is taken on a stretcher to the mosque or straight to the burial place where prayers may be said by an imam. Burial is usually without a coffin. The head is turned to face Makkah. Muslims are never **cremated**.

## Judgement

Muslims believe that there will be a day of judgement when God will bring everyone back to life and judge them. God will decide on who will go to heaven and hell depending on how many good and bad things they have done in their lives. For Muslims, heaven is called Paradise.

Muslims also believe that God is kind and merciful, and will forgive a bad person if he or she is truly sorry for what they have done.

➤ This 16th-century illustration shows the Mughal emperor Babur instructing his workmen about the planning of a new garden. The Qur'an says that Paradise is like a perfect garden, a place of peace and happiness. Many Muslim rulers have tried to design gardens similar to the ones in Paradise, as described in the Qur'an.

◄ A Muslim cemetery in Singapore. All Muslims are buried facing Makkah.

## In our own words

"When I die, I will be buried. Then the angels will ask me three questions. 'Do I believe in God?', 'Do I accept Muhammad ﷺ as his prophet?' and 'What is your book?' If I answer correctly, then I will wait until the Day of Judgement. I'll be told whether I'll be going to Paradise or Hell."

# 5★ Islam today

Today, Islam is seen by some people as being at odds with the Western world. But Islam strongly encourages its followers to respect and accept other people.

## Women in Islam

Islam teaches that men and women are equal, but different. Women are responsible for the family. Like men, women have the right to be educated and have a career, to participate in political life and to own property.

In modern times, there are many well known women politicians. Benazir Bhutto, Pakistan's former Prime Minister, Sheikha Hassina, former Prime Minster of Bangladesh and Tansu Çiller, former Prime Minister of Turkey, are just three examples.

## Dress

The Qur'an teaches that both men and women should dress modestly. While men usually keep themselves covered at least from the navel to the knees, women must be covered from head to foot, showing only their wrists, feet and face.

**weblinks**

For more information about Islam in the modern world, go to www.waylinks.co.uk/series/religiontoday/Islam

◄ *Benazir Bhutto was elected Prime Minister of Pakistan in 1988. She was the first female leader of a Muslim state.*

## The hijab

The hijab is a veil that covers the head and shoulders. It is worn by some Muslim women. Here, four Muslim women explain their choice:

"People think I'm forced to wear the hijab by my parents. I'm not. I want to wear it. I have more confidence in myself."

"We don't wear the hijab all the time. We don't wear it at home when there are just family members around. This is what the Qur'an says."

"If you wear a hijab, nobody says, 'Buy this, buy that, you're supposed to look like this'. I don't have to worry about buying things that are 'cool'."

"I've just started working in a bank. I'm allowed to wear the hijab at work but I choose not to. I like the freedom and the chance to dress like the other girls at work."

▼ *Most of the people who live in Turkey are Muslims. Some of the women sitting on this seafront in Istanbul wear the hijab; others wear Western dress.*

## Conflict

On 11 September 2001, **terrorists hijacked** four planes and crashed two of them into the World Trade Center buildings in New York, USA, destroying the buildings and killing nearly three thousand people. The terrorists were Muslims who were working for Al-Qaeda, an Islamic terrorist group. Since then, Islam and terrorism have often been linked.

Islam teaches that violence is wrong and that it is wrong to hurt the innocent. But it also teaches that it is right to defend the Muslim faith when it is attacked.

## Fundamentalism

Fundamentalists are people who believe that holy books (such as the Qur'an) have to be followed to the letter in every way.

In the last thirty years, many Muslims have become angry. They feel that the West has interfered too much in their countries. They want to go back to traditional Islamic values. This fundamentalism is different in every country. In Iran, women can drive cars and have jobs. When fundamentalists were in power in Afghanistan, women did not have the right to go to school.

There are also problems between Muslim groups. Sunni and Shi'ah Muslims have been fighting each other for many years in Iraq.

◄ A woman holds posters asking for 'shari'ah law' in Jakarta, Indonesia, in February 2004. The word shari'ah means the 'way' or 'path' to be followed by all Muslims.

▲ *Members of different faiths sometimes meet to try to understand one another better. Here, Christians, Jews and Muslims gather for a Ramadan meal at the Islamic Center of America in Detroit, USA, in December 2001.*

## Looking ahead

For eight hundred years, Muslims led the world in science and learning. Then Muslim countries lost their power and were taken over by Western nations. Many Muslims are still angry about this and have tried to make Islam stronger. Others are keen to make peace with the West and to live according to their faith.

### In our own words

*"My favourite verse from the Qur'an is, 'Oh mankind! We created you from a single (pair) of a male and a female, and made you into nations and tribes, that you may know each other (not that you may despise each other).'"*

# Glossary

**Arabic** The language which comes from Arabia, in the Middle East.

**ayatollah** A leader of Shi'ah Muslims.

**colonies** Parts of a country that are taken over by another country.

**cremation** The burning of a body after death.

**crusades** Christian wars against Muslims during the Middle Ages. The purpose was to take Jerusalem.

**fasting** When people do not eat for religious reasons.

**hijack** To take over a group of people with violence, often while on an aeroplane.

**Hindus** Followers of Hinduism, a religion that developed in India.

**idols** Statues or images worshipped as gods.

**imam** A Muslim (man) who leads prayers in a mosque.

**immoral** A person who is not moral. Someone who knows the difference between right and wrong, and chooses to do wrong.

**Ka'bah** The cube-like building in the middle of the Great Mosque of Makkah. It is said to be the first house built for the worship of God by Adam.

**khalifah** One of the early leaders of Islam.

**martyrdom** The act of dying for one's faith.

**mosque** A building where Muslims go to pray.

**pilgrimage** A journey to a holy place.

**prophet** A person who brings messages from God, often about the future.

**Qur'an** The Muslim holy book. The word Qur'an means 'recitation'.

**sacrifice** When something is given up or offered to God.

**scribe** A person in ancient times whose job it was to write down the letters and documents of his rulers.

**Shahadah** The most important Muslim belief: 'There is no god but God and Muhammad ﷺ is his Prophet'.

**Shi'ah** Muslims who believe that the true successor of the Prophet Muhammad ﷺ was the fourth khalifah, Ali, and the eleven other imams after Ali.

**successor** The person who takes over a post or a job when the person holding that post dies.

**Sunnah** The life, thoughts and sayings of the Prophet. It includes the Hadith and the Sirah.

**Sunni** Muslims who believe that the first four khalifahs were the true successors of the Prophet Muhammad ﷺ.

**terrorist** Someone who tries to make a political point with violence.

# Timeline

| CE | |
|---|---|
| c.570 | Birth of the Prophet Muhammad ﷺ |
| 595 | The Prophet marries Khadijah |
| 610 | The Prophet is first visited by the Angel Jibril |
| 622 | The Prophet flees to Madinah; Muslim calendar dates from this year |
| 630 | Muhammad ﷺ takes control of Makkah and throws idols out of the Ka'bah |
| 632 | Death of the Prophet; Abu Bakr becomes first khalifah |
| 634-44 | Umar is second khalifah |
| 638 | Muslims conquer Jerusalem |
| 644-56 | Uthman bin Affan is third khalifah |
| 656-61 | Ali bin Talib is fourth khalifah |
| 732 | By this date Muslims rule entire area from Spain to India |
| 1099 | Christian crusaders conquer Jerusalem |
| 1187 | Muslims under Salah-ad-Din retake Jerusalem |
| 1301 | Founding of the Ottoman Empire |
| 1526 | Founding of Mughal Empire |
| 1857 | British capture of Delhi, India |
| 1858 | End of the Mughal Empire |
| 1918 | Collapse of the Ottoman Empire |
| 1926-32 | Establishment of the united kingdom of Saudi Arabia |
| 1947 | British rule ends in India; Pakistan is created |
| 1995-2001 | Fundamentalists called the Taleban rule Afghanistan |
| 2001 | Terrorist attacks on New York and Washington, USA |
| 2003 | Iraq is invaded by US troops. The President, Saddam Hussein, is captured. Sunni and Shi'ah Muslims begin to fight for control of the country |

## Further reading

*Religions of the World: Islam* by Sue Penney (Heinemann, 2003)

*A Year of Festivals: Muslim Festivals Through the Year* by Anita Ganeri (Franklin Watts, 2003)

*Introducing Religions: Islam* by Sue Penney (Heinemann, 2006)

*Beliefs and Cultures: Muslim* by Richard Tames (Franklin Watts, 2005)

# Index

Abraham (Ibrahim) 5, 9, 20, 28, 31
Abu Bakr 8, 10
Afghanistan 44
Akbar 13
Al Hijrah 8, 9, 26, 27
al-husain ibn Ali 11, 26
Ali bin Talib 10, 11
Allah 4, 7, 17
Al-Qaeda 44
angel Jibril 4, 7, 16, 18, 26, 28
Arabia 6, 14
Arabic 4, 10, 17, 19, 23
Arabic numerals 38
arts 39
Ashura 11, 26, 27
astronomy 38, 39
ayatollahs 11
Babur 13, 41
Bhutto, Benazir 42
Bismillah 17
British Empire 13, 14
calendar 8, 9, 26, 27
caliphs, see khalifas
charity 36
China 5
Christians 12, 13, 18, 45
Çiller, Tansu 42
clothing 18, 28, 30, 34, 35, 42, 43
crusades 12
death 40, 41
divorce 34
Dome of the Rock 12
family life 32-35
fasting 21, 28, 29
festivals 26-31, 33
Five Pillars 21, 22, 30, 36
food 21, 28, 45
fundamentalism 44
Ghar Hira 7
Hadith 19
hafiz 20

Hajj 27, 28, 30-31
handwriting 39
hijab 43
Hijrah, see Al Hijrah
Hindus 14, 38
Hussein, Saddam 14
Id-ul-Adha 26, 27, 28
Id-ul-Fitr 26, 27, 28, 29, 33
imams 11, 36, 40
India 5, 13, 14
Indonesia 5, 29, 44
inventions 39
Iran 5, 11, 44
Iraq 11, 44
Jabal al-Nour 7
Jerusalem 12, 26
Jesus (Isa) 5, 20
Ka'bah 8, 9, 23, 25, 30, 31
Khadijah 6
khalifahs 10, 11, 12, 17
khateeb 25
khutbah 25
Kuwait 14
Laylat-al-Mi'raj 26, 27
Laylat-ul-Qadr 26, 27
Madinah 8, 9, 18, 26
Makkah 4, 6, 7, 8, 9, 18, 26, 27,
   28, 30, 31, 40
marriage 34-35
mathematics 38
Maulid al-Nabi 26, 27
mihrab 24, 25
minarets 24
Moses (Musa) 5, 20
mosques 6, 8, 24, 25, 26, 28, 30,
   36, 39, 40
mu'adhin 24
Mughal Empire 12, 13
Muhammad, Prophet 4, 6-8, 10, 11,
   16, 18, 19, 20, 26, 28, 30, 31, 32,
   37, 39

Noah 5, 20
oil 14, 15
Ottoman Empire 12
Pakistan 5, 11, 13, 14, 21, 22-23,
   34, 42
Paradise 41
pilgrimage 9, 21, 27, 28, 30-31
prayer 22-25, 28, 29
prophets 5, 20
Qur'an 4, 7, 10, 11, 16, 17, 18, 19,
   20, 21, 22, 23, 26, 28, 30, 37, 39,
   41, 42, 43, 44
Ramadan 26, 28, 29, 45
rashidun 10
salah (prayer) 21
Salah-ad-Din (Saladin) 12
Saudi Arabia 4, 6, 14, 30
scientists 39
Second World War 14
Shahadah 20, 21, 32
shari'ah law 44
Sheikha Hassina 42
Shi'ah Muslims 11, 26, 44
Sirah 18, 19
sufis 15
Sunnah 11, 18, 19
Sunni Muslims 11, 44
terrorism 44
Turkey 5, 12, 42, 43
Umar 10, 12
Uthman bin Affan 10, 17
Western influence 14, 15, 35, 44, 45
whirling dervishes 15
women 24, 25, 37, 42-43, 44
World Trade Center 44
wudu 23
Zaid ibn Thabit 17
zakah 21, 33, 36-37